A is for adorable, which describes Gabriel each and every day.

B is for **brave.** Gabriel doesn't let fear get in the way!

C is for **creative**, that is uniquely you.

D is for dreamer, that keeps Gabriel true!

E is for **eager** to learn new things each day!

 is for **fantastic**. Which describes Gabriel in every way!

G is for giving, that is a kind thing to do.

H is for Gabriel hugs.
that keep others from
feeling blue.

I is for imagination, pretending is best!

J

is for joy, that Gabriel brings to all the rest!

K is for **kindness** the greatest way to be!

L is for laughter. Sweet special giggles for Gabriel and me.

M is for magical. A fun way to play!

N is for noble. The way we all strive to stay.

O is for one-of-a-kind.
That is definitely you!

P is for priceless which Gabriel is that too!

is for quirky, so silly and fun!

R is for remarkable. Gabriel is remarkable from moon until sun!

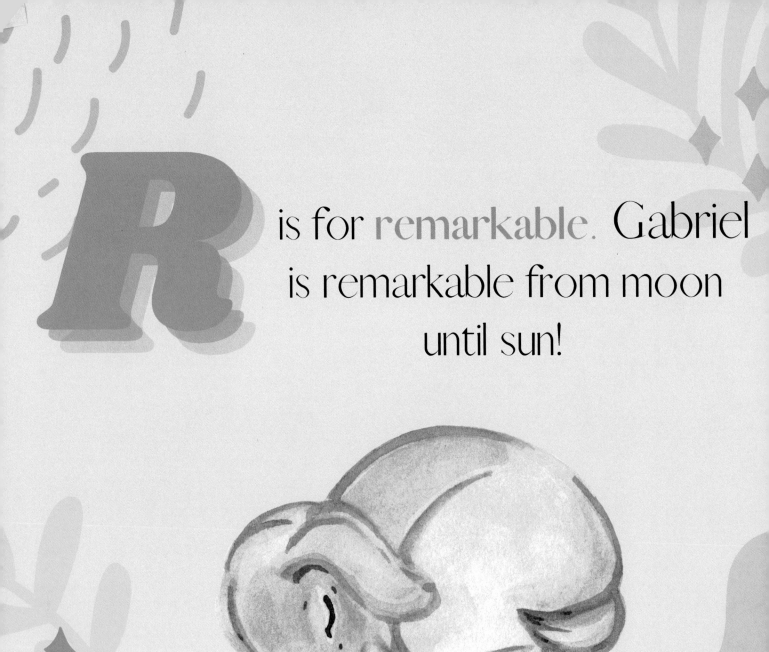

is for special, like you
are to me.

T is for together, my favorite way to be.

U is for **unique**, Gabriel that has always been you!

V is for vibrant, the way your heart shines so true.

W is for **wonder**, while I watch you grow.

X

is for eXcited, to see what you know.

Y is for YOU, to know exactly who YOU are.

Z is for zig zags, I take for you whether near or far.

Gabriel
I love you
from
A - Z
Love,

———————————

Made in the USA
Middletown, DE
29 November 2022

16428490R00015